Bulldogs
The Essential Guide

ROB DUFFY SERIES EDITOR

Published in Great Britain in 2019 by
need2know
Remus House
Coltsfoot Drive
Peterborough
PE2 9BF
Telephone 01733 898103
www.need2knowbooks.co.uk
SB ISBN 978-1-91084-367-3
Cover photograph: Adobe Stock

Contents

Introduction

So, you have recently brought an adorable English Bulldog into your home as a new family member or are considering doing so. In this book, we will delve into all information English Bulldog! As the national dog of England, the English Bulldog is much beloved by many. While they were originally bred for bull-baiting over 500 years ago, that aggressive part of them was eventually bred out, and the modern English Bulldog is one of the gentlest breeds around. Bull-baiting and dog-fighting were banned in England at one point, and breeders started choosing dogs with bigger heads and shorter legs. Bulldogs may appear fierce, but they are the friendliest dogs around. These lovebugs are well-known to have supreme patience with children and are surprisingly great with other animals, including cats. They are low energy dogs and do not require a ton of exercise. English Bulldogs are also known to look as great as seniors as they do as pups as they 'hold their beauty.'

Man's best friend can be a valued member of your household and bring companionship and joy. Studies have shown that having a dog can be good for your health! Having a dog can get you out of the house for exercise. While out exercising your dog, you can meet other proud dog owners and increase your social circle. Science has also confirmed that owners of dogs usually are less stressed out, often because of the affection and cheer they receive from their dog. Dogs, especially funny English Bulldogs with their endearing underbites, are always waiting for you eagerly when you come home with bright eyes, a wiggling bum, and a happy attitude. Who else would be this excited and happy to see you even if they just saw you 1 hour before? The great personality of the English Bulldog is contagious. These dogs bond with the whole family and are very companionable. You have made an excellent choice.

Things to Know About Owning A New English Bulldog

While owning a new dog can be exciting it can also be perplexing at times, and there are many considerations for owning a dog, whatever the breed. Here are a few top tips to get you started and some further insight into the English Bulldog breed. This is one special breed indeed.

Microchip

There are numerous decisions to be made with your English Bulldog. One such decision is whether to microchip your dog. Most dog charities urge dog owners to microchip their dog to help the dog be reunited with their owner if the dog becomes lost. All around the world, there are issues with stray dogs. This is not just due to dogs being dumped. It is partly because there is no way to reunite lost dogs with their owners without proper identification. If you microchip your dog and they get out, and someone picks them up, it is likely either the vet, animal warden or charity that picks your dog up will be able to reunite you with your beloved pet. One quick scan for a microchip and your information pops up. English Bulldogs are sought-after purebred dogs. If someone steals your English Bulldog, then it will be good to have that identification.

Most dog charities urge dog owners to microchip their dog to help the dog be reunited with their owner if the dog becomes lost.

Vaccinations

As a new dog owner, you will want to keep in mind that your dog will need vaccinations and regular check-ups with the vet. This is an added, but necessary, expense on top of daily food and water. Vaccinations are important which we will discuss further in the first chapter. Make sure your dog's vaccinations are kept up as recommended as it could literally save their life. Do keep an eye on your English Bulldog after vaccinations as English Bulldogs can tend to be a bit agitated after vaccinations and there is a small possibility of an allergic reaction. They are sensitive to vaccinations. Many English Bulldogs have become very sick after the Bordetella (kennel cough) vaccine If you think anything is off, call your vet.

Pet Insurance

Pet insurance is another option to consider. Most pet-insurers do not cover pre-existing health conditions or vaccinations. There are a few that do. It is important to look up several insurers online and check to see what they cover for the amount you will pay each month. However, if your dog needs an unexpected operation, pet insurance can come in handy as many people cannot afford to pay such a large sum at once. You will need to think carefully about whether you could afford an unforeseen large vet bill if it came up.

English Bulldogs are prone to some health issues such as major respiratory problems, severe skin allergies, arthritis, overheating, acne, eczema, dry skin, hip dysplasia, degenerative spine disease, idiopathic head tremors, cherry eye, joint and ligament injuries, vomiting, regurgitation, heart disease, fold dermatitis, Brachycephalic Airway Syndrome, and vaccination sensitivity. English Bulldogs also have the highest rate of cancer of most breeds. It would be good to have your pet insured before anything like this can possibly show up. These things happen, and it is good to be prepared.

Weight

Obesity in dogs is on the rise these days. English Bulldogs are more prone to obesity than some other breeds as they have low energy levels. They also are prone to food allergies. It is important to figure out what you will be feeding your dog. Also, if your dog starts to gain too much weight as an adult, you need to know what to do about it. Avoiding feeding your dog kitchen and table scraps is one good way. Also, having a regular feeding schedule can be effective. Many times, people give their dogs treats to make their dog happy. Sometimes, instead of a treat, a good petting or brushing can make your dog feel like they have received a treat and it is a good bonding experience between you both.

Exercise

Exercise is very important for all dogs. English Bulldogs need the exercise to keep fit and not gain weight. You need to know how much exercise your English Bulldog will need. Other than walks, you will need to know what other forms of exercise you can give your dog to keep its heart rate up to burn off energy and calories. Most people do not know that it is not good to over-exercise and English Bulldog. This type of care for your dog will be explored further in this book.

Food

Sometimes it can seem complicated knowing what is okay and what is not to feed your English Bulldog. There are many foods that can make your dog ill or even kill them. Chocolate is not the only dangerous food, although it is the most talked about. It can be challenging to keep your dog from eating human food, especially if there are other members of your household around such as children. Some foods that may seem harmless, like caffeine, raisins, and grapes can get your dog very sick. It is important to let children know not to feed the dog anything without asking you first.

Health

Your English Bulldog's health can become a confusing matter. Such as the fact that English Bulldogs get chilly very easily and are sensitive to hot and cold weather. They can be sensitive to vaccinations and so forth. There are vaccinations that are needed at certain times in a dog's life, not just when they are puppies. You also need to know when your dog will need worming. Flea and tick control for your dog are very important as fleas and ticks can make your dog ill. Some ticks can even get humans ill. It is also good to know some basic doggie first aid to use before you bring your dog to the vet for a hurt or cut paw.

A New Family Member

This book has a lot of information that you will find helpful and useful when owning an English Bulldog. This will assist you in taking the best care of your English Bulldog so that you can have a fulfilling life together. These helpful tips will help you feel more confident with your beloved new family member. Having a canine friend in your family, especially a friendly English Bulldog, can help you build many fond and happy memories.

2

The English Bulldog Puppy

Getting a puppy sounds like a cute and fun idea. English Bulldog puppies are beyond adorable with their little underbites and can be lots of fun. It is good to keep in mind the practical aspects of having one. Puppies need a exercise, a lot time, attention and care. Socialising puppies is very important also to keep them from being anxious or badly behaved when they meet other dogs. English Bulldogs are one of the most amiable breeds out there. They become very strongly bonded with their owners. It must be a snub-nosed breed thing, but they do best if not left alone too long. They can become destructive if left on their own for long periods of time. English Bulldogs can be very stubborn when they do not want to do something. They do, however, respond well to persistent and patient training. There will be work involved. Also, keep in mind that English Bulldog puppy exercise needs to be done in moderation as too much strenuous activity like running up and down stairs, really long walks, and jumping up on chairs can give them joint issues. Free-running in the garden is a good start. Then, once they are fully vaccinated, start lead walking on the grass and then move to harder surfaces. Also, they need regular cleaning of the cute little wrinkles on their faces to avoid a condition called skin fold dermatitis. They are so darn cute though and for many English Bulldog owners, worth the work.

> Puppies are known to chew and eat almost everything in sight. This is especially true of English Bulldog puppies. You need to get the chewing under control when they are pups, or it will carry on as a bad habit as adults.

Time to puppy-proof your home

Puppies are known to chew and eat almost everything in sight. This is especially true of English Bulldog puppies. You need to get the chewing under control when they are pups, or it will carry on as a bad habit as adults. You will need to puppy-proof your home which means getting pretty much any item they can chew out of your pup's way. Besides teething, English Bulldogs will usually start destructive chewing if they are having separation anxiety, if they are bored or to release stress.

- Make sure to move away any rugs you might have on the floor. Puppies will chew on them and drag them around.

- Any small objects such as keys, coins, marbles, jewellery, needles, pens, screws, pins, buttons or tiny bouncy balls need to be kept away from pups as they can swallow them. This can be dangerous as they can choke or need a visit to the vet to remove the items if they get stuck in their digestive tract.

- As with small children, you need to literally lock away medications and cleaning products. Keep them up where your pup cannot reach them as they can chew through containers.

- Until your puppy is trained not to jump up and take food, it is important to not leave food on countertops or tables as your puppy will steal it. Young English Bulldogs might not be able to reach these items, but it is better to be safe than sorry as something may just fall off of the counter.

- Any heavy objects that can be knocked over need to be taken away from the area your pup is in. A heavy object falling can cause serious injury to your English Bulldog puppy.

- Puppies tend to chew everything, and that includes electrical cables. Keep them away by putting them in a cable tidy, or you can use sturdy masking tape to tape cables to the wall.

- Please make it clear to your children that they cannot leave chocolate anywhere that a puppy can get to it. Chocolate has been known to kill both adult dogs and puppies.

- If your home has a garden, it needs to be properly fenced as some pups can jump higher than you might think. English Bulldogs are not huge jumpers but make sure your fence is high and sturdy enough that they cannot get over it.

- Put up a child gate to keep your pup from going into rooms in your home that may hold toxic or dangerous items.

Getting your puppy settled

While it can be exciting for you to bring a new puppy home, your pup will need some time to settle in. Your home is a new place for them, and they have just met you. It will take a bit of time for things to become familiar to your pup. It is crucial to your pup's well-being to help them settle into your home in their early days there. Your English bulldog pup may be easily frightened and nervous. There have been a lot of pups given away because their owners could not handle them. Do your best to help your pup be as comfortable and calm as possible. Once your English Bulldog gets used to your family, they will be very loving as they love people. These are definitely people dogs!

Give your pup their own space

It's a great idea to give your pup some space that just belongs to them. Sort an area of your home that is only for them and will be where they will sleep. You can mark the area by putting down a chew-proof dog bed there along with some toys. Pups need to have appropriate toys to help curb their chewing instinct. Place your pup in the bed and give them a positive acknowledgment like "good pup." You can also give them a little treat. Tell your puppy to "stay" and use a certain hand gesture like you are telling someone to halt. If your pup stays, then reward them with another little treat. Incorporating hand gestures is good for when your dog cannot hear you but can see you. It is good to get little bite-sized treats so as not to over-feed when teaching your pup. These positive words and little treats are known as positive reinforcement. English Bulldogs can be very sensitive to your tone of voice and harsh words. How you speak with your dog will have consequences that are long-lasting in both how your English Bulldog reacts to you or listens to you. Keep things positive!

Family meet & greet

When you bring your little English Bulldog pup home to meet the family make sure everyone is calm, and the pup is not overwhelmed with everyone coming at the little darling all at once. Gentle introductions, one person at a time, are important. Each person can choose to stroke the pup softly or let the pup sniff their hands. Another good introduction is letting the pup come up to people on its own. It is very important to teach children how to interact properly with the pup. They should never pull the pup's tail (though some English Bulldogs just have little nubs of tails that are hard to grab) or come at the pup from behind. It is vitally important that children are taught never to go near a puppy or dog when they are eating. Other behaviours, for children with pups, that are a no-no are grabbing, poking, or lifting the dog up.

Anxious pup

Some puppies, when they are taken from their siblings and mother, get something called separation anxiety. Give your pup some good attention and cuddles to give them assurance that all is well. There are also special collars called DAPS collars that are used by dog charities to calm puppies and anxious dogs when they are sent to new homes. The collars duplicate the pacification pheromone that is like the smell of the mother dog. The DAP means 'dog appeasement pheromone' and additionally can be purchased and applied as a diffuser spray. Some people have found these effective in dogs with separation anxiety or to prevent it when a dog or pup goes to a new home.

At first, your pup will follow you everywhere. Hence the saying "follows me like a puppy dog." However, you need them to start feeling comfortable when they are not in the same area as you. If you do not start this early, they will get into the habit of barking or crying when they are by themselves. A child gate comes in handy in this instance as they can see you through the gate but cannot follow you everywhere. If you try this for several days, stretching out the minutes they are not with you each time, it is a good start. Next, you can put them in a room or area with one of their toys for five or ten minutes and close the door. When you leave, do not make a big deal out of leaving.

Puppies grow twenty times faster than adult dogs and need to be fed often to keep up with that growth.

Helpful hint

To help keep your pup from getting separation anxiety, make a point to not fuss over your puppy each and every single time you are near them. Don't praise them and give them eye contact and cuddles every time you see them or are near them. They will get used to this. If you make a big fuss over them every single time you see them, they can get stressed when you suddenly do not and have other things to do. That said, English Bulldogs still cannot be left alone for hours on end, or they can get destructive. They need to be with their people.

Puppy food

Puppies have different feeding schedules than adult dogs. English Bulldog pups need to eat four times per day until they are 16 weeks old. From four to six months of age, your English Bulldog pup should eat three times per day. They grow twenty times faster than adult dogs and need to be fed often to keep up with that growth in their first months. They also need different nutrition in their food. Puppies need more fat, protein, and certain minerals than adult dogs do. Growing and developing takes up a lot of energy. After they are 24 weeks old, you can reduce meals to twice a day for the remainder of their lives. Bulldogs should be fed out of a flat bottom pan with straight sides. Use a stainless steel pan as it lasts longer and has less bacteria than a plastic bowl. It is always important to have fresh water available for your English Bulldog puppy. Good, clean water is essential to your pup's health. It is so important not to overfeed your English Bullgdog. They do not need the extra weight as it makes it more likely they will get health problems. They are stocky dogs and do not need more pressure on their short legs. .

Helpful hint

It is best not to change what you feed your puppy often when they are young as it can upset their stomachs and possibly cause diarrhoea. Puppies have sensitive stomachs in their early months. If, for any reason, you do need to change what they are eating it is best to do it slowly, adding a bit of the new food at a time. If your English Bulldog is having a food allergy, however, discuss the best way forward with your veterinarian.

Toys and chews

Puppies have a need to chew, especially when they are teething. Getting the proper toys for chewing is much better than ending up with your furniture or other belongings chewed to bits. English Bulldogs are chewers. There are many toys and chews on the market that are made especially for puppies. Some examples are:

- Puppy-sized Nylabones
- Chews that preferably crumble when bitten
- Soft Toys
- Kong puppy toys you can hide a treat in
- Teething ropes for pups
- Chilly bones that you can freeze to help soothe your pup when teething
- Squeaky plush toys
- Puppy frisbees

House training your pup

House training your pup can seem daunting. It can be difficult but rewarding when it is all over with. With consistency and patience, your pup will be house trained before you know it. When a pup eats, its digestive system is stimulated. Most pups will defecate within 30 minutes of eating and will urinate within about 15 minutes of eating. Puppies need to urinate at the very least every hour or two as they do not have the same bladder control adults do. If a puppy is excited, it can urinate suddenly. Therefore it is a good idea to take your puppy out often to urinate if it has been exploring, active or playing. Basically, in the first days of your pup coming home with you, your pup will need to have toilet breaks every 20 minutes or so. Be consistent and be patient and your English Bulldog will catch on.

- After your English Bulldog pup has woken up, eaten or had a drink, it is important to take them outside after. If they urinate or defecate, give them praise while they are doing the action. It is good to say the same thing each time in a happy voice like 'good pup going wee wee!' or 'good pup going poo poo!' You can also give them a pat on their head. If they don't do anything, then ignore them. They will soon learn that they are supposed to do their business when you take them out at these times.

- Keep an eye out for when you see your puppy might need to toilet. Many times, they will start looking around worriedly and pace looking for a corner or hiding place to go. If you see this behaviour, ask them if they need to go to the toilet and take them out right away. Choose what words you will use for urinating and defecating and stick with the same wording. Then your dog will catch on to what you mean.

- It is best, when house training your pup, to take them out to the same spots they have gone to the toilet before. They will usually recognise their scent and realise that is the place to go.

- There can be times, when training your pup, that they may need to go to the toilet and you are not around. Lay down puppy pads (they look like squares of nappy) or newspaper on the floor in your home (usually where there is tile or linoleum). When your pup has used these to urinate or defecate on, give them praise. Puppies thrive on praise. If they go elsewhere in your home, ignore them. Puppy pads can be purchased from pet shops and vets.

- Each day move the puppy pads closer to the door. Then out to the garden. Pups know their own scent and are likely to do their business where they have gone before.

- If your pup messes in the house, you need to clean it up right away to make the smell go away. It is usually best to use a special carpet cleaner to do this. These can be usually found at pet stores or some markets. If your pup can smell where they urinated before, they may do it again in the same spot.

- Pups need to go to the toilet much more often than adult dogs. This is like human babies and adults. They cannot control their bladders properly until they are adult dogs. Remember to take them out as late as possible at night and first thing in the morning. If your pup has become excited, then take them out. Any time they have eaten or have been drinking water you need to take them out. They will get through this puppy stage before you know it and will need to go out less often!

Do not forget that this breed is sensitive and takes it very personally when someone treats them harshly, which results in them avoiding you. It can take time for their feelings to mend if you are harsh. Positive reinforcement is always the best approach when training an English Bulldog.

Helpful hint

If you punish your pup for toilet accidents, they have in your home it is not good. This can make your pup frightened to go to the toilet in front of you at any time- even when you are outside. Ignore them when they do this. Praise them when they go on the puppy pad or outside.

Your pup and teething

At between four to five months old, your English Bulldog puppy will begin the process of losing their baby teeth. You may find tiny little teeth around the house or on their pet beds. Their teeth will slowly grow back in, and most English Bulldog pups should have a full set of adult teeth by the time they are 12 months old. During this teething time, pups can want to chew a lot of things, and it can be a difficult time for both your pup and you. The tips below should help:

- Your puppy will bite you often when they are teething. When puppies do this to each other the other pup will yelp when the first pup bites it too hard. This will usually surprise the biting pup, and they will release. You need to imitate this yelp or say loudly "OW!" and let your hand go limp when your pup bites you. When your pup lets go of your hand, then ignore them for about 20 seconds and then start playing with them again. If this happens more than three times in 15 minutes, then it's time to stop playing for a while. This teaches your pup that rough play stops, and that gentle play can keep going.

- When your English Bulldog puppy is teething, they will feel the need to chew constantly. It is important to buy them toys that are especially for teething pups. Kong toys for puppies that are teething are perfect as they are hard to destroy.

- Brushing your pup's teeth can help and will get them into the habit of having their teeth brushed while also soothing their tooth areas. Make sure only to use toothpaste specially made for dogs. Human toothpaste is not good for dogs. Choose a dog toothbrush that is soft.

- Tell your children to keep stuffed animals out of the way as your pup will use this chewing compulsion to tear them apart and you will have fluff everywhere!

- A good low-calorie snack that can help with chewing is a carrot. Keep them cold in the fridge to help with soothing. There are also rope toys that you can wet and freeze to soothe your pup's mouth.

Brushing your pup's teeth can help and will get them into the habit of having their teeth brushed while also soothing their tooth areas.

Puppy training

Puppies need more than just house training. Proper behavioural training is important for puppies and will carry on into their adulthood if you are consistent. Dogs you see that are well-behaved were not born that way. They have had training. I cannot emphasise enough how important training is. However, I must reiterate, English Bulldogs are sensitive despite their tough-guy looks and will be hurt if you speak harshly to them. It really is not the way to go and can set back training. English Bulldogs are independent, stubborn, and when they don't want to do something they can put their paw down. They also are super cute. So, it can be a little more difficult to train them. They are so darn cute that you may giggle at them when they are acting out a bad behaviour. You have to have the right amount of being firm without being too harsh when it comes to training English Bulldogs.

Puppy obedience

It is vital that you use the same words for your commands for your dog. If at one point you say 'stop' and the next time you use the word 'stay' your English Bulldog will not associate it with the same action and your pup can get confused. It is also best to use just one word for your commands. For example, just use the command 'stay' rather than 'stay there.' Also, this is a good time to train your puppy to chase a ball or toy and bring it back to you. Praise them when they bring the toy or ball back to you. Later, this will be great exercise for them.

When you give your command, avoid shouting as this can excite or startle your pup. You need to use a firm, clear voice and be as patient as possible. Be consistent with your wording and keep a calm head. Patience is key with training.

Recall command

One of the most vital skills for a dog to know is recall. You want your dog to come running to you whenever you call for them. It is important to practice this every single day. You can start this training in your home simply by calling your puppy to you using his or her name. Repeat this at random times throughout the day. You can also do this in the safety of your fenced garden if you have one.

The next step is calling your pup to you on a short lead outdoors. Once they start coming to you each time with the short lead, then try a long lead for this exercise. It is good to have a pocketful of little bite-sized treats and give them one each time they come back to you when you call their name. Remember, start pups walking on grass and then later on concrete to protect their joints.

You want your pup to associate coming back to you with being a good thing. Never scold, yell at or scare your dog if they do not come back right away. Doing so will have your pup associating coming back to you with a bad experience, and they will be a lot more likely not to come right back to you. You really need your English Bulldog to come back to you when you call them to avoid dangers. If they run into a street, a car may not see them in time. Also, if they run up to a big dog that is aggressive, they could get really hurt. Recall is essential.

Vet visits

It is very important to keep up-to-date with your puppy's health. Make sure to find a reputable veterinarian before you get your pup. It might even be a good idea to ask a potential vet how much experience they have with snub-faced breeds like your English Bulldog. It is highly advisable that you find a vet that has a lot of experience with Bulldogs. It is not good to scatter for a vet last-minute if something happens. Ask friends, rescue groups or breeders for recommendations. Your English Bulldog is part of the family, and the veterinarian will be your pup's doctor. You want someone who knows what they are doing.

Vaccines

Check your puppy's health book to see what vaccinations or treatments have been given. You do not want to double-vaccinate your pup or de-worm it too close to a previous treatment. With English Bulldogs being sensitive to vaccines, this could be fatal. Bring the vet book with you each time to your vet. The first vaccination a puppy receives is when it is eight weeks old. It is called a five in one as it starts to build up immunity to 5 different diseases:

1 Distemper (a serious virus that attacks the digestive, respiratory, and brain/nervous system of dogs)

2 Adenovirus type 1 (hepatitis which can cause severe liver dysfunction and even death)

3 Adenovirus type 2 (a respiratory disease that can turn into pneumonia and can be fatal)

4 Parainfluenza (a respiratory disease that can give your puppy kennel cough)

5 Parvovirus (this viral disease is very serious, highly contagious among unvaccinated pups and is usually fatal)

Three weeks after the first set of vaccines your pup will get their second series of the five in one. Then, another three weeks later they will receive their third series of five in one vaccination. At 14-16 weeks of age, your pup will receive their rabies vaccination. Until your puppy has had all their vaccines, they should not be out and about. They should stay in your home and garden until this is complete as they can catch these illnesses out in the general public. It is always good to double check this information with your veterinarian. Again, some English Bulldogs are very sensitive to vaccines so keep an eye on them after and call your vet if something seems off. There have been many incidences where English Bulldogs have had nearly fatal reactions to the Bordatella (kennel cough) vaccine. Discuss this with your vet.

Worms, fleas, and ticks

When a puppy is born, it has worms. Most pups are wormed at around three weeks of age. Make sure to check with your veterinarian to see how often your pup will need this treatment. If pups are not given worm treatments, and they have worms for a series of time, it makes them very ill. Ask your vet what the appropriate flea and tick control would be for your puppy's age. Fleas and ticks can cause health issues for your beloved puppy. However, using a dose for an adult-sized dog can make your pup gravely ill.

More about vet visits

Your vet will check your dog's heart, teeth, coat, temperature, ears, and eyes during a check-up. They will also keep track of your puppy's weight to see if they are growing properly. Vets should go out of their way to make this as good of an experience as possible for your pup. This is especially important for English Bulldogs as they may have more vet visits than some other dogs due to being prone to health issues.

3

The English Bulldog Teenager

As your puppy becomes a teenager, you will have different matters to deal with. Will you have your dog spayed or neutered? Will you invest in micro-chipping your dog? Will you make sure to socialise your English Bulldogs with other dogs to keep them well-rounded? What happens if they get loose and go walk-about while you are taking them out on a walk? One good thing about English Bulldogs is that, when they are properly socialised and trained, they can easily get on with other family pets. However, they might be aggressive with dogs they do not know. They are good with most children and are wonderful family pets. English Bulldogs also make good watch dogs! They love to be near their people. As previously mentioned, it is not good to leave them alone for long periods of time, or they can get behavioural issues.

Dog Socialisation

After all of their vaccinations are sorted, and the vet gives you the okay to take your dog out in public it can be both exciting and a bit scary. Your dog could get into a fight with another dog or be aggressive with other dogs. These instances are precisely why your dog needs to be socialised with other dogs as early as possible once they are cleared for their vaccinations. It is important that both your dog and you can sense body language in dogs you come across. This will let you both know whether a dog is being playful or if there is something more aggressive going on. You need to learn about the dog greeting ritual.

Dog Greeting Ritual

Dogs sniff each other when they meet, especially for the first time. This greeting is a way of saying 'hi' to each other. Sometimes this even extends to sniffing each other's rear ends, but this is perfectly normal. There are times when one dog will react badly with their body tense, and they can even go for the other dog. In this case, the hair on their back may stand up, and their ears will bend back. Other times the dog will give a lively bark and can bounce around in circles or lie down submissively.

Once the dogs have sniffed each other, they will either become interested in each other or just go along their merry way. Dogs that are interested might wag their tail, bark joyfully, light-heartedly jump on the other dog or even lick their face. You can also be a part of this ritual by reaching out your hand slowly for the other dog to sniff. It is always best to ask the other owner if their dog is friendly and okay with people before doing this. If the owner says it is ok, and the dog seems fine after sniffing your hand, then you can give the dog a pet. If the dog looks frightened or backs away, then give the dog its space and do not try to pet them.

Dogs sniff each other when they meet, especially for the first time. This greeting is a way of saying 'hi' to each other.

Doggie socialisation

It is very important to socialise your dog properly. You do not want your dog attacking other dogs. Here are some tips:

- Make sure your dog is on a lead when you meet a dog you do not know. Ask the owner if their dog is okay with other dogs. If yes, then let your dog approach the other dog for the sniffing greeting ritual. It's never okay to just let your dog run over to another dog without asking the owner if it is ok, especially if the owner has their dog on a lead. The dog may be on a lead for a reason such as aggression or other behavioural problems.

- Sometimes the other person's dog will growl or bark. This does not always mean it will attack. You will soon learn the difference between a friendly bark or a 'keep away from me' bark.

- Some signs of aggression or fear from the other dog can include hunkering down with their head low, and the fur standing up on their back or the dog's body will stiffen completely, and they will stand very still. These signs can mean it is possible the dog will attack.

- Just as there are some humans who do not get along well, there are some dogs that just might not end up being friends. You can't make your dog like another dog. Some encouragement is good, but it is not good to try and force the matter.

- Another great way to socialise your dog and give you some social time is to find another dog walker to go on walks with you. Your dog will learn how to be with other dogs, get great exercise and start socialising! Since your English Bulldog cannot go on really long walks it is good to match up with someone whose dog goes on shorter walks also.

Spay or neuter?

When your dog is of age to reproduce it is a good time to think about getting them neutered or spayed. Some dog owners feel that it is un-natural to spay or neuter their pet. Other owners, like breeders, want their dog to have puppies. The most widespread view is that it is a much healthier choice to neuter or spay dogs.

Reasons for spay/neuter

- If you spay your female dog, they will not have to experience being on heat. When a female is on heat, usually she will need to be confined to the home and garden or just get short walks to avoid them falling pregnant.

- It is typical for a female dog to go on heat twice per year. This normally happens every six months. When a dog is on heat, they can become moody, aggressive and restless because of the changes in their hormones. These heat cycles can last as long as three or four weeks.

- Spaying your female dog can lower their chances of getting urinary issues, ovarian disease, and some cancers.

- With male dogs, neuter can help reduce the chance of them getting prostate issues, hernias, and aggression toward people and other dogs. It also reduces issues with them spraying (inappropriate urination) and eliminates the chances of getting testicular cancer. Most of the time you can prevent leg humping in male dogs if they are neutered.

- Another benefit of neutering your male dog is that it will stop them from chasing around females on heat. Un-neutered male dogs have been known to dig out of gardens or jump fences to find their way to a female dog on heat.

- Most experts will agree that it is healthier for your dog to be spayed or neutered.

The cons of spay/neuter

- For breeders, spay and neuter is a con as they will not be able to breed new dogs.

- Spay/neuter is not an inexpensive operation. However, some animal rescues offer vouchers for discounts.

- Spayed/neutered dogs can put on more weight. If you feed your dog a healthy diet and give it plenty of exercise this can be cured. Ask your vet how much food they recommend for your dog.

- Some people worry about their dog being put under anaesthetic for the surgery. Anaesthetics these days are much better than they used to be and usually, the benefit of spay/neuter outweighs the risk of the surgery. However, anesthesia in English Bulldogs can be riskier than in other pets. Bulldog sedation and anesthesia safety are critical to ensure a good outcome. This is when having a vet who is very experienced with English Bulldogs and snub-nosed breeds is very important.

Unsettling news

Thousands of dogs and puppies are dropped off at charities like Dogs Trust and the RSPCA every year. Many times, it is because their owners cannot properly take care of them or because they no longer want the responsibility. This problem is magnified by the fact that there are so many unwanted puppies born due to lack of spay and neuter. Many animal charities, local authorities, and vets offer discounted or free spay or neuter for dogs to help prevent this problem.

What is the recommended age for spay/neuter surgery?

You should spay female dogs as early as four to six months of age before they get their first heat.

Most vets usually agree that male dogs can be neutered as early as six months of age and it is best before 12 months of age. You should spay female dogs as early as four to six months of age before they get their first heat. This is in the UK. In the USA and Australia, they spay and neuter much earlier and some vets in the UK are leaning this way. For older dogs, speak with your veterinarian about any possible risks of surgery.

How does spay/neuter surgery work?

- The reproductive organs of female dogs are removed in spay surgery. The testicles of male dogs are removed in neuter surgery.

- The night before the surgery your dog will not be able to eat after a certain time as they want your dog to be on an empty stomach for the surgery for safety reasons. It is important to follow the vet's instructions as to when is the latest you can feed your dog the night before.

- Your English Bulldog will need a check-up at the vets before their surgery to make sure they are fit for the operation. While the operation is being performed, your dog's vital signs will be watched. Depending on the time of the surgery, your dog may need to stay overnight.

- Your dog should not be in a lot of pain after the surgery. Males tend to bounce back much more quickly than females. There will be some discomfort. Your dog will want to lick the wound. Try to get them not to. Some vets will give you a cone to put around their neck to avoid licking. If anything seems off, call your vet right away. It is better to be safe than sorry.

Keep an eye out for the following:

- If your dog is still lethargic after a couple of days, call your vet for advice.

- If the incision turns a nasty shade of purple or red, if it starts to open, or if anything oozes out of it contact your vet right away.

- The incision area may swell some. If you feel it is severely swollen, then contact your vet right away.

Is spay/neuter surgery safe?

These surgeries are routinely done every day. For the most part, they are very safe. However, with any use of anaesthesia or surgery, there is a tiny risk that things can happen. Spay and neuter procedures are routine for vets, and they do them a lot. So, your vet would be very experienced if anything were to happen. Speak with your vet about any questions you may have.

When can I breed my dog?

You need to ask yourself if you can make sure that each puppy you breed will find a good home. If you cannot guarantee that, then it might not be a good idea to breed your dog. A litter of puppies sounds like a fun thing, but it is a lot of work keeping up with them. You have to clean their mess, keep an eye on their health, make sure they get wormed and have vaccinations. It is a costly endeavour both timewise and financially. Think twice and do your research before attempting to breed your dog. Reputable English Bulldog breeders have done their research and know which dogs to mix with which. It is not just a matter of finding another English Bulldog to make puppies with.

Why microchip my dog?

Microchipping is highly recommended by dog charities as it is a safe way to reunite lost dogs with their owners. Some reasons for this are:

- Microchipping works to reduce the number of stray dogs. When a stray dog is taken in by a dog warden, vet or charity it is checked immediately for a microchip. If the information on the chip is up to date, the dog can be returned to its owner.

- Microchipping your dog ensures that you can prove you are the rightful owner. This is especially important if someone steals your dog and claims it is theirs. Microchipping helps reduce dog theft

- It is relatively cheap to microchip and register your dog. Some groups even hold events for free microchipping. The RSPCA has done such events in the past.

Behavioural issues

You've done the pupping training, and it may seem like the training work is finished. Sometimes behavioural issues still happen. Below are some of the issues that happen most often and some ways to remedy them. Also, it is always good to keep training up with your dog to exercise their mind.

Mounting other dogs

Spayed/neutered dogs mounting other dogs has very little to do with sexual behaviour. It is about dominance. If your dog is mounting another dog from behind and both are spayed/neutered, it is all about dominance. Females do this too. It is not just males. Most times the mounting dog is trying to tell the other dog it is the boss. This problem should go away on its own. However, if it provokes fights repeatedly, you should consult a professional dog trainer.

Lead pulling

No one likes their dog yanking their arm while they walk. This is one of the top reasons that dog owners decide to take their dog to a trainer or obedience school. English Bulldogs can be a bit stubborn, as we mentioned before. Sometimes teaching them this part is tricky. Firstly, you need to figure out which side of your dog you will walk on and stay with that side each time you walk. You will want to hold the lead in the hand opposite to the side he/she is walking and have a little treat in the hand closest to him/her and let him/her see it. As you start to walk slowly, your dog will hopefully follow your hand. Each time they do this say the word 'heel' to them and give them a tiny bit of the treat. Keep repeating this as you walk along saying the word 'heel' as your dog walks behind or beside you.

Snapping and biting

Snapping or biting is one of the worst things your dog can do, and it needs to be corrected as soon as possible. Both small and large dogs can hurt someone with a bite. Even though an English Bulldog is not a huge dog, it can do some serious damage with a bite. Biting and snapping need immediate attention.

- If you are giving your dog a treat and your dog snaps at you, stop right away and do not give them the treat. This lets them know they will not be rewarded for bad behaviour.

- If you and your dog are playing and you receive a bite from your dog of any kind, stop the play immediately. This lets your dog know that the fun stops when they bite.

- If one dog bit another dog, the dog on the receiving end would growl. Do this if your dog bites you. Growl at them.

- Make sure your dog has chew toys to bite as they might just be bored and start biting.

- This is good for everyone in the family to know. Never suddenly wake a dog that is sleeping as their instinctive reflex could be to bite.

Bad recall

If your dog has not mastered recall (coming to you when you call their name), it can drive you up a wall and be very stressful. Dogs have teenage phases and may try and pull a strop. Keep up the training advice given for puppies in the first chapter. Be consistent, and your dog will start to listen. Remember, do not punish dogs for not coming to you as that can make them more likely to not run to you in the future when called. It is important with English Bulldogs to keep up this training as they can get seriously hurt if they do not come back when called and run into a street or toward an aggressive dog on a leash.

Barking when you are away

Canines are pack animals. They consider you and your family their pack, and they like to be with their pack. Unfortunately, no human being can be home 24/7. Some dogs get some separation anxiety and bark when you are gone. This can be because of loneliness, boredom or sheer anxiety. You need to help your dog get used to being on their own for periods of time when you cannot be there. Remember though; English Bulldogs are not bred to be left alone for long periods of time. It is not good to leave them alone longer than a few hours at a time. Here are some ways to help with separation anxiety:

- Believe it or not, leaving your radio or television on while you are out can help your dog not feel so lonely as they hear human voices.

- Leave a safe toy or chew for your dog when you leave. One great idea is a Kong toy with a treat inside to keep them occupied trying to get it out.

- When you leave, do not make a huge fuss over your dog.

- When you are home, you will need to ignore them for part of the time and not be attentive all of the time. It shows them that you will not be making a fuss of them always just because you are home.

- Leave an old sweater or shirt of yours in your dog's bed. Your scent will reassure them. Before you leave the house, make sure to take your dog out to go to the toilet. If your dog is inside your home with no way to get out, they will get anxious if they need to use the toilet.

- If you are not home enough with your English Bulldog, then they may become destructive. They may also chew things and bark a lot. It can become a bad situation. If you do not have time for an English Bulldog, then you should not adopt one. If you feel you are not home enough, then maybe hiring a dog walker to come check on your English Bulldog in the day, while you are at work, is a good idea. Also, families that have people home at various times are good as it staggers the time that your English Bulldog is alone.

Professional help

If you have persistent behavioural issues with your dog, it is important to consult with a dog trainer, your vet or a special canine behaviourist. There is a great website called **www.apdt.co.uk** where you can click on 'local dog trainers' to learn more about professional dog trainers in your area. APDT stands for the Association of Pet Dog Trainers, and each member of this group is vetted. It has been around since 1995.

Books for additional learning

There are so many good dog training books out there. One that is really good is *The Dog Whisperer: The Compassionate, Nonviolent Approach to Dog Training* by Norma Eckroate and Paul Owens.

4

Exercising & Feeding your English Bulldog

English Bulldogs are low energy dogs and sleep 14 hours per day on average. They do not need as much exercise as other dogs, but they do need more than you might think. Also, as we mentioned before, they have a tendency to be overweight if you are not careful. Feeding your English Bulldog properly and making sure they get plenty of exercise is key to having a healthy and happy dog. There are many different types of dog food, and it can get overwhelming and confusing figuring out which is best. English Bulldogs are known to have food allergies. It can sometimes be best for them to eat a special food made for the Bulldog breeds. This will delve into some helpful hints for feeding your beloved English Bulldog, and we will also give advice on exercise.

Feeding schedule

It can be hard to sort the exact right amount of food to feed your beloved pet. What is the best food? How many calories are too many calories? There are so many different kinds of dog food these days. Which is the right one?

There are also choices between feeding your dog wet food, dry food or both. Some people feed their dogs a special raw food diet. Some owners mix a dry food mixer into their wet food. Mixers should not be fed on their own. They do not have the complete nutrition needed, hence the title 'mixers.' They are meant to be mixed with regular dog food.

Dry food

Most people are familiar with dry food for dogs. It comes in kibbles and is a complete food for your dog. It is considered good for your dog's teeth as it requires chewing. There are so many different kinds of dry food. They even have special varieties that are for older dogs, obese dogs, and puppies. There are even dry foods made especially for English Bulldogs as they have special mouths with their underbites.

Wet food

Wet food is a complete food also and is usually in a foil tray or in tins. Keep an eye out for preservatives, food colourings and flavourings. If possible, it is best to go as natural as possible without a lot of additives as they have been known to cause health issues for dogs in the long run.

Mixers should not be fed on their own. They do not have the complete nutrition needed, hence the title 'mixers.' They are meant to be mixed with regular dog food.

Is the BARF diet for your dog?

An alternative diet, called the BARF diet is getting some notice as more people are using it. It is supposed to be more like a natural diet for your dog than kibbles. The meat used is all raw. So, the bacteria that are usually killed through cooking is still there. Cattle these days are given a lot of drugs, such as antibiotics, which can cause issues with dog health. It has been said that eating raw meat like this can turn some dogs aggressive as it replicates how they would eat in the wild.

Helpful hint

Just like humans, dogs can have allergies to some ingredients in dog food. For example, some dogs are allergic to wheat and need a wheat-free food. Things to look out for are dry skin, itchy skin, and lethargy. Check first that fleas are not the issue. There are special dog foods for dogs with food allergies. Ask your vet or pet store to help point them out for you. English Bulldogs are notorious for food allergies to certain foods or ingredients. There are special foods just for Bulldogs that avoid possible allergens and reduce flatulence.

What is the right amount of food?

Most dog food containers have feeding guidelines based on your dog's age and size. The right amount of food depends on how much exercise your dog gets, your dog's age and their weight. If you are unsure of what would work best for your pet, it is a good idea to speak with your vet or a knowledgeable pet store owner. Many dry foods will come with a measuring scoop that you can use to make sure your dog receives the correct amount of food. Trays and tins will let you know portion size also. If your dog has had extra treats on a certain day, you should reduce how much other food you feed them on that day. English Bulldogs should eat their food out of a pan with straight sides and a flat bottom. Stainless steel containers are preferred as they have less bacteria than plastic ones.

How many times per day to feed your English Bulldog

Generally, it is best to feed English Bulldogs twice per day after the age of six months. Some people feed their dog once per day. The good thing about twice a day is that they do not go hungry waiting 24 hours for their next meal. Twice per day feeding is best for English Bulldogs. English Bulldogs are prone to bloat, but any dog can get bloat. This is a condition that commonly affects dogs with barrel chests and small waists like English Bulldogs. Bloat is caused by over-feeding, over-hydrating and exercising your dog too close to feeding times. Bloat is dangerous. When a dog has bloat, their swelled out stomach twists within their body which puts pressure on other organs. If you see the following signs, get your dog to a vet immediately as bloat can be fatal. Even minutes can make a difference in saving your dog's life. Some signs of bloat are:

- Hard stomach
- Very swollen stomach (bloated to the sides)
- Dog trying to vomit but just retching instead
- Pain in the tummy area when touched
- Restlessness and panting

When feeding your adult English Bulldog twice per day, it should be in the morning and early evening. It is best not to feed your dog right after or before they exercise. English Bulldogs are known for being very greedy eaters. Eating a lot too quickly and getting too much air in can cause bloat. Slow feeder bowls, which can be purchased online or from your pet store, stop them from eating so quickly. Also, do not let them drink a large amount of water right after eating. It is also best to refrain from feeding your dog table scraps as some foods we eat are not good for dogs, and also too many snacks can make your dog obese.

It is important to always have plenty of fresh water available to your dog at all times other than right after they eat (because of bloat dangers). Your dog should have a special eating area where they will not be disturbed while they eat. Some dogs develop food aggression if people get in the way of their food. Make sure that children are warned to stay clear of a dog when they are eating as dogs can snap when bothered while they are eating. A bite is a bite and can be damaging.

Obese dogs

People tend to want to give their dogs lots of treats and food as an act of love. However, it can cause obesity in your English Bulldog as they are prone to have issues with their weight. Some reasons obesity is bad for your dog are:

- Obese dogs have a higher risk of heart disease and diabetes just as obese humans do.

- If your dog is overweight, it can add fatty tissue to their heart and put extra pressure on the heart. If a dog is carrying too much extra weight, it's heart can just stop at some point.

- Many overweight dogs start to suffer from arthritis and other joint problems.

- Carrying that extra weight can give them breathing issues.

- As you would with a child, you need to learn when to say no to too much food for your beloved dog if you want them to stay as healthy as possible and live a good life. Dogs, especially English Bulldogs, will eat endlessly if you let them and it is up to you to be a responsible dog owner to make sure they are not overfed.

- If your dog is obese, they will not be able to play and run around with other dogs which is a shame.

- Any extra weight on your English Bulldog can be extremely hard on their joints and expose them to so many health issues.

Keeping the weight off

- Keep treats to a minimum. When training your dog, use the tiny little treat bits and eventually move to praising them with a good head rub for doing the right thing.

- Human food has a lot of sugar and salt that is not good for dogs. Don't hand your dog food from the table.

- When you have the urge to give your dog a treat, try to substitute that treat with a nice rub down or brushing for you dog. Hey, we all like massages. Your dog will like a quick one too.

- Dogs need exercise. Exercise your English Bulldog to help them stay happy and healthy! Exercise should happen regularly and daily. Make sure to keep up with walking your dog.

Keep treats to a minimum. When training your dog, use the tiny little treat bits and eventually move to praising them with a good head rub for doing the right thing.

- Exercise is not just in the form of walks. Dogs like to do other things for exercise too. Some English Bulldogs love to chase balls or toys that you throw for them too. This is great exercise even in the garden where you throw their ball for them over and over to wear them out!

- It is important for dogs to socialise with other dogs. It helps give them extra exercise and satisfies their need to be with their own kind.

If you are doing all you can to help your dog keep at a healthy weight, yet the pounds keep piling on, it is important to speak with your vet. Your dog could possibly have a health issue like an underactive thyroid which is treatable with medication.

How to tell if your dog is overweight

Sometimes it is not completely obvious if your dog is overweight. Many times, since owners see their dog every day, they do not notice slight changes in weight. Have any of your friends mentioned your dog might be packing on kilos? Sometimes people who have not seen your dog in a while will notice weight gain more. Also, while some people think it is cute that dogs are fat, it really can shorten the dog's lifespan.

Each time you take your dog to the vet have your dog weighed. If your vet is telling you that your dog is overweight, they will know what they are talking about as they have been trained to know these things. It is important to listen to your vet in these matters to keep your dog healthy. Owners sometimes make excuses saying how much their dogs love their treats. They forget that it can shorten their dog's lifespan being overweight. Dogs also love cuddles and petting which, as we mentioned before, can be used as a treat.

Here are more ways to tell if your dog is overweight:

- With full-grown dogs, an obvious way is if their collar has become tighter. This does not apply to growing dogs or puppies. English Bulldogs develop and grow slowly. Most English Bulldogs reach their full height by the age of twelve months. They are fully grown in muscularity by around 18 months or even as late and 2 and a half hears of age. Most of an English bulldog pup's bones fuse between 9 months and 12 months old, but the bones in their elbows and legs may be developing until they reach around 18 months old.

- If your dog's belly hangs down, then this can be due to extra weight.

- If your dog seems to breathe heavy a lot, this could be due to weight gain. It is always best to check with the vet when it comes to heavy breathing as it could be another issue.

- If it is difficult to feel your dog's ribs, because there is fat over them, this is an obvious sign of being overweight.

- If your dog does not want to exercise much, this can be an indicator. Again, if this starts to happen and keeps up, it is good to check with your vet to make sure there are no other issues.

Oh no, my dog is overweight!

Don't freak out if your dog has become overweight. This can be reversed with effort. Do not cut their food in half right away as it can be a shock to their system and is not healthy for your English Bulldog.

- Slowly switch over your dog's food to an easy-to-digest food that is low in fat. Start adding it in slowly with the food you are already feeding to not give your dog an upset tummy from a fast change in diet.

- Speak with your veterinarian. They may know of a certain food that has worked well for other patients or some kind of special diet you can use to help your dog lose weight.

- Definitely cut back on treats and switch to low-fat treats.

- As with humans, to lose weight, your dog needs to burn more calories than he or she eats. That means an increase in exercise. If your dog loves to retrieve you can sit back and throw a ball for them a zillion times until they are worn out as an add-on to walks. Remember though do not let your English Bulldog exercise for too long in one go and definitely not in high heat.

- A helpful website to refer to is **www.petsgetslim.co.uk**. It shows even more ways to help your pet lose weight.

Why is my dog not eating?

English Bulldogs love to eat. If your dog is not eating, there may be an issue with their health. Contact your vet to bring your dog in for a check-up to get to the bottom of this. When a dog does not eat it can be serious. It is always best to be safe than sorry and at least call the vet. There are times when a dog is just a finicky eater, and all you need to do is change their food.

Doggie Exercise

Dogs love to get out for exercise. Even lower energy breeds like English Bulldogs like to get out for a trot. They need to release their energy! It is important to find just the right harness or leash for your walking buddy.

Different kinds of harnesses and leads

- You can use a traditional lead for your English Bulldog, but it is not recommended as, if they pull too hard they can injure their necks. They are prone to breathing issues. So, other options might work better.

- Harnesses are great for English Bulldogs. It is simpler, with a harness, to control your English Bulldog without choking them. A harness keeps pressure off of their necks. English Bulldogs are prone to breathing issues as previously mentioned.

What is the right amount of exercise for my English Bulldog?

Dogs can become depressed, act out and gain weight if they do not get enough exercise. Just how much exercise is enough?

In addition to toilet walks (if you do not have a garden your dog does his or her business in) your English Bulldog will need a minimum of two 20-minute walks per day. Create at least 20 but no more than 40 minutes a day for exercising your adult English Bulldog. This may mean letting your dog into the backyard or bringing them to a park to move around. Either way, the physical activity should be restricted to around a half hour to forty minutes total total. They should also have some free access to a secured garden, if you have one, to run around some. Throwing the ball and having your dog retrieve it over and over is good additional exercise but do not over-do it as you do not want your English Bulldog getting heat exhaustion. If your dog is being destructive at home, they may not be getting enough exercise.

> Dogs love to get out for exercise. Even lower energy breeds like English Bulldogs like to get out for a trot. They need to release their energy!

Mental exercise

Physical exercise is not enough. Dogs need mental stimulation. For this we suggest:

- Giving your dog a challenging toy like a Kong that has low-fat treats inside. It can take your dog a long time to figure out getting the treats out, and this mentally stimulates them.

- Bringing toys, a ball or a frisbee to switch things up on walks if you have an open area for them to play.

- Using special tug toys to play tug with your dog.

Heat exhaustion in English Bulldogs

Any dog can get heat exhaustion or a heat stroke. Due to the English Bulldog having a shorter breathing system, they are at a much higher risk of heat exhaustion. This shorter airway makes it harder for English Bulldogs to draw air into their body to cool. The only place dogs sweat is through their foot pads. So, panting is the main way they reduce built-up body heat. Do not leave your English Bulldog in a car on a warm day, even a mildly warm day (24 to 27 degrees Celsius). Radiant ground heat can also overheat your dog. Put your hand to the sand, road, or pavement. If it is too hot to keep your palm there comfortably, then it is too hot for your English Bulldog. Older and over-weight English Bulldogs are even more at risk for heat exhaustion and heat stroke.

Heat exhaustion can turn into heat stroke if your dog is experiencing:

- Loss of consciousness or fainting

- Wobbling or staggering when they walk

- Weakness

Once your dog is at this point it is an emergency, and you need to cool your dog down right away:

- One person can get on the phone with the vet but the other needs to start helping the dog immediately.

- Rinse your English Bulldog with cool water- not freezing cold water. DON'T try to make your dog drink as they can vomit up the water and it can go into their lungs.

- Use an ice pack on your dog's head. You can also soak towels in cold water and apply it to your dog's body.

- If the option is available, put your dog into a tub of cool water. Nothing too deep as the English Bulldogs cannot swim.

- Your dog's airways will be swelling as they pant which will make them pant even harder. Children's Benadryl allergy medicine can be given by dropper. Ask your vet in advance or via the phone what the right dosage is. You can also ask your vet about having a supply of injectable Benadryl on hand for these cases. It is always best to be prepared.

- Keep this going until your dog's body temperature is near normal and then get them to the vet ASAP. If possible, do the things mentioned above while en route to the vet while someone else drives.

- Remember, when you might only feel as mildly hot, it can be too hot for your English Bulldog. When the weather is hot, make sure to limit your English Bulldog's time outside. It is important they have a constant supply of clean, fresh water to drink from and a shaded area to rest. You need to stop playtime before it over-taxes your English Bulldog.

Important note

English Bulldogs cannot swim well without a well-fitting and approved life vest or life jacket. Their big heads, heavy bodies, and short legs make it impossible for them to keep their heads above water without a life preserver. These dogs will sink. Within seconds they can drown if they fall into water that is deeper than they can stand up in. NEVER leave your English Bulldog unsupervised near water above their head. Basically, do not leave them alone near water that is deeper than 10 or so cm. You can supervise them in a kiddie plastic pool to cool off as they are prone to over-heating. You can also take them swimming with you, but they need the life jacket and need you with them at all times.

5

Dangerous Foods for your English Bulldog

There are many dangerous items for dogs in your home if they are eaten by your English Bulldog. We will go over some of those and what you should do if your dog eats some of the banned list items. Keep in mind that English Bulldogs have breathing issues already. If they get a dangerous food stuck in their throat, they can die.

Chocolate – the biggest no-no

One of the most dangerous foods for dogs is chocolate. Most dogs will have a bad reaction to eating chocolate, and it is not worth the risk giving it to your beloved English Bulldog. There is a compound called theobromine in chocolate that is made for humans. It can kill dogs even in smaller doses. There is a special chocolate for dogs in supermarkets and pet stores that does not contain this compound. However, this can be confusing if you have children in the home who may not understand the difference.

If my dog has chocolate what should I do?

Don't panic if your dog eats chocolate. The poisoning caused by chocolate in dogs is usually built up over time. If your dog just had a small amount, they should be ok. However, you should always call your vet for advice to be on the safe side. If your dog has eaten a lot of chocolate, then rush them to the vet immediately, calling ahead to let them know you are coming. If your dog gets medical care quickly enough then hopefully their life will be spared.

What does chocolate poisoning look like?

A dog that has been poisoned by chocolate will usually have diarrhoea and vomit. You may see chocolate in the vomit. Your dog may be even more hyper than usual, and if you touch their stomach, they will react as if in pain. As the poisoning goes on, they may have issues with walking and may shake and twitch. Some dogs even have convulsions. It may take hours after your dog has eaten the chocolate for them to get these symptoms as chocolate can take a while to digest.

How to treat chocolate poisoning

If your dog has not already vomited, their veterinarian may give them something to make them vomit. If they have been vomiting repeatedly then they will be given a drug to stop the vomiting. Your vet will next give your dog something like charcoal to absorb the poison. Intravenous fluids will be administered to keep your dog from getting dehydrated. Unfortunately, chocolate is not the only food item that dogs should not eat. There are other kinds.

Coffee and tea

Caffeine is not good for dogs, and it can cause a poisoning like chocolate does in dogs.

Onions

Onions can cause anaemia in dogs due to a toxic chemical they contain and can cause breathing issues with your dog.

Raw Foods

Giving your dog raw egg used to be thought of as being good for their coats. However, it's best not to feed your dog raw eggs as they could end up with salmonella. Also, keep away from giving your dog raw meats like liver without cooking it as raw foods like liver can contain destructive bacteria like antibiotic-resistant salmonella.

Milk

Dogs can be lactose intolerant just like humans. Some symptoms of this are when they have smelly farts or their stomach bloats. It's best not to feed your dog milk, especially if they have these symptoms.

Bones

There is the old saying 'give a dog a bone.' It is normal for people to think of giving a dog a bone. Many bones can be dangerous for your dog, however. Chicken bones can poke and stick in your dog's throat which can make them choke. The chicken bone can even puncture their lungs! With larger-sized bones they can break and lodge in your dog's throat, choking them. If you do want to give your dog a bone, make sure it is not cooked as cooked bones splinter more easily. There are a lot of alternatives to bones, like rawhide bones and chews, that are safer for them to chew and gnaw on.

If a bone gets stuck

You can try removing the bone with your thumb and two fingers to pull it from your dog's mouth. Putting your fingers in your dog's mouth to make them gag helps if the bone is further down. You may, however, get bitten. It is best to contact your vet for their advice on what to do if a bone is stuck.

Cheese

Cheese should not be given to dogs in large amounts. It can give them diarrhoea and give them issues with their pancreas.

Sultanas, raisins, and grapes

A majority of dogs cannot digest sultanas, grapes, and raisins. If they eat them, they can have renal failure. There have been dogs who have ended up dead after eating just a few grapes.

Alcohol

Your dog's heart and the central nervous system can be affected by alcohol. In some cases, alcohol has killed dogs. Keep alcohol away from your dog.

Xylitol

It has been found out that a sweetener called Xylitol that is found in many sugar-free food items like biscuits, mints and chewing gum is toxic to dogs. This sweetener is found in sugar-free foodstuffs, like chewing gum and biscuits

Here are some other items to keep away from your dog:

- Human medicines – keep the locked away up high!
- Rat poison and anti-freeze

- Weed-killer (do not put weed-killer down on your grass if your dog is likely to eat the grass!)
- Human vitamin supplements

If your dog has any of these call your vet's emergency number right away. Keep hydrogen peroxide 3% around as it can be used to induce vomiting if your vet recommends that. Bring the bottle of whatever your dog has ingested. Even if your dog looks fine get them to a vet right away if they have had any of these bullet-pointed items.

6

First Aid for your English Bulldog

Unfortunately, things happen, and your dog may become ill or get injured at some point. They may pull a muscle or cut their paw, and you need to know what to do before you get them to your vet's practice. This has some good advice, but it is best to call your vet for their professional opinion.

Keep a first aid kit for your dog

Humans are not the only ones who need first aid kits. Your pets are part of the family also, and it is best to have a first aid kit ready in your home, just in case.

What items should I put in the doggy first aid kit?

Having a bottle (or two) of a sterile, pressurized saline "wound wash" in your pet's first-aid kit is a great idea.

- A tick removal tool (you can find these at pet shops). Also, a pair of tweezers for stings, thorns, and splinters.

- A dog boot as mentioned earlier in the book. These are made of a special material that stops your dog's hurt paw from getting water on it. Mikki hygiene dog boots are great for keeping away infection when your dog gets a paw pad injury. You can find these in pet stores or online.

- Hydrogen peroxide, the 3% solution. Hydrogen peroxide can also make your dog vomit if they have eaten something they should not if your vet asks you to make them vomit.

- Having a bottle (or two) of a sterile, pressurized saline "wound wash" in your pet's first-aid kit is a great idea. It's a fast way to do a thorough initial cleaning of your pet's wounds because it quickly generates the pressure necessary to remove fragments and extricate bacteria from the damaged tissues. Don't use hydrogen peroxide to clean the wound as it kills helpful cells that help heal the wound.

- Surgical tape and bandages.

- A paper that shows how do the Heimlich manoeuvre and CPR is a good addition to your first aid kit. This can be really helpful in an emergency.

- Ask your vet for a recommendation of an antihistamine to put in your first aid kit in case your dog has an allergic reaction to something like a bee or wasp sting.

- It is good to include a flea comb in your kit.

- Special dog antiseptic cream you can ask your vet for. Human antiseptic cream can be too strong.
- In case your dog needs medicine broken up into their food, a pill crusher is a good item for your kit.
- It is good to put a warm blanket in your kit in case your dog needs it if they fall ill.
- Keep a couple of syringes in your kit for liquid medicine for your dog.
- Ask your vet for an anti-inflammatory for dogs for your dog first aid kit in case it is needed. Make sure to ask your vet for the proper dosage.

First aid for dogs

Try to keep your mobile phone on you when out with your dog in case of emergencies. However, sometimes emergencies happen where you will not be able to speak with your vet first. It is good to know some basic first aid.

Possible broken bones

If it looks like your dog has broken a bone, please call your vet ASAP.

If your dog gets hit by a car

It can be shocking if your dog is hit by a car. You need to pick them up carefully. You cannot leave them on the road of course. It is best if you can get help lifting your English Bulldog. Don't hug your dog as it can cause more pain. There may be broken bones and internal injuries. If you can lay them on a flat surface, it is best (something like plywood board). You can lay them on a blanket, if not, and then have someone help you lift them into the car.

- You want your dog's body as stable as possible when lifting it or you can make the pain a lot worse.
- It is best if you have someone help you lift your dog and go on the drive to the vet. One person can drive while the other pets and soothes the hurt dog. If you have no one else, then just get the dog to the vet ASAP.

- Sometimes your vet will come out to you if your dog is hurting too much to be moved. Your dog may need a sedative or pain medication before moving their body.

Cut paws

- Check your dog's paw to see if there is anything in it like grass seed, dirt, nails, glass or anything else. Having your tweezers is good if something like a sticker is embedded in the cut.

- If there is a broken paw, it will need trimming to keep it from getting snagged on things which can aggravate the paw wound. Take your dog to the vet if the claw is broken off at the base.

- You need to clean your dog's paw. Use either an antiseptic wipe or lukewarm water. Also, you can use sterile, pressurized saline "wound wash" from your pet's first-aid kit. It's a fast way to do a thorough initial cleaning of your pet's wounds because it has the pressure necessary to remove fragments and also get bacteria out from the damaged tissues.

- You can use dog antiseptic cream if you have it from your dog first aid kit. Don't use human antiseptic cream.

- If the cut is large, then wrap the paw with a bandage. If you have a special dog boot, then put it on your dog. If not, then wrap the paw with a plastic bag.

- Check the wound often. Take your dog to the vet right away if you see signs of infection (discharge, swelling, extreme redness.)

- If the bleeding of the cut just won't stop then apply sterile gauze pads and put pressure on it. The bleeding should cease after 10 or 15 minutes.

- If it is just a little cut, then it does not need a bandage as the fresh air will help it heal. However, you need to clean the paw each time your dog goes outside and comes back in.

- After using these first aid methods, if you are still worried then take your dog to the vet. Your dog's health is the most important thing.

When your dog swallows something wrong

Take your dog to the vet immediately if they swallow something they are not supposed to. X-rays can be done at the vet to see what may have been swallowed. Some items can pass through your dog's system, and they will poop it out naturally. Other items can cut your dog's internal organs like their stomach and will need to be removed with surgery. Vets have experience with these operations.

A dog attack

If your dog has been in a fight with or has been attacked by another dog, you should check your dog right away for any injuries. If your dog seems hurt, you should call your vet. Some signs of injury include yelping, walking awkwardly, or bleeding. There may be internal injuries you are not aware of.

If one dog attacks another, the owner can be liable if the attacking dog is not wearing a collar/harness or was not on a lead and the attacked dog was. The police can be called in such situations. Sometimes dogs just get in a fight, and it was no one's fault per say. It is always good to have a discussion with the other owner before acting. Keep in mind you both will have adrenaline running from breaking up a dogfight. Try to keep your cool.

Diarrhoea

With diarrhoea, it is important to check if there is blood in it. Some small amount of blood once or twice is normal due to straining to poo. If there is a lot of blood or if you are seeing blood regularly then call your vet immediately.

The best way to stop diarrhoea is to not feed your dog for 24 hrs. Make sure there is plenty of fresh, clean water available. This gives their stomach some time to settle, and then you can give them some rice with some boiled chicken (you can pour the boiled chicken broth on the rice but let it cool some.) The rice should help stop the diarrhoea. Always call your vet if you think something is really wrong and need advice.

Usually, the quickest way to give your dog pills is in some food. Sometimes with capsules, this will not work, or your vet may advise they take the pill on an empty stomach.

Giving your dog pills

Usually, the quickest way to give your dog pills is in some food. Sometimes with capsules, this will not work, or your vet may advise they take the pill on an empty stomach. Other times it will not work in food for some reason. You can also try:

- There are special canine tablet pockets or tablet biscuits made specifically for you to hide pills inside of.

- There is a pill-gun you can use which will hold the pill, and then you release it down your dog's throat. Follow the instructions carefully that come with the pill-gun or ask your vet to demonstrate.

- You can put a pill in a bit of cheese but keep this to a minimum as human food is not good for dogs. Cheese can also cause gas and English Bulldogs already are prone to being gassy.

Fireworks issues

A lot of dogs are scared of fireworks. It can send some of them into a panic, and many dogs have been known to jump fences or even jump out of windows when scared by fireworks. If your dog is severely distressed by fireworks these tips may help:

- A dog that gets severe distress from fireworks should not be left home alone on holidays where fireworks will be let off. If you have to be away, it is good to get a dog-sitter or take your dog to kennels.

- When you are home with your dog during fireworks, play some music or put on the television to drown out some of the fireworks noise.

- If you need to take your dog out for toilet breaks, make them quick and hold on tight to their lead as fireworks may startle them.

- If your dog's firework phobia is severe, there are sedatives your vet can provide or suggest. Valerian tablets or Dorwest Herbs Scullcap have no side effects, and you can get them from pet shops directly.

What if a vet is unaffordable?

If you fall on hard times and have a low income, there is a charity called PDSA that have free veterinary treatment available. In order to qualify you need to live in the area of a vet or hospital and receive council tax benefit or housing benefit. For more information go to their website at **www.pdsa.org.uk**. While it is free, a donation is usually helpful.

Vet services for those on means-tested benefits or low incomes are also available through The Blue Cross. They even have ambulances that will help you bring your animal to the vet if you are housebound. A small donation is asked for to keep the charity going. It is mostly for housebound and older adults who cannot get their pet to a vet on their own. Go to **www.bluecross.org.uk** for more information.

If you are on benefits, Dogs Trust might offer free or discounted spay or neuter for your dog if you live in specific areas. Sometimes there are discounted, or free vaccinations or spay/neuter months run by local authorities or councils. If you do not qualify for help, it is good to ask your vet if they offer payment plans.

If you have not adopted a dog already, you should really think hard if you will be able to afford vet bills and all that having a dog entails. It is more than just food and walks, especially since English Bulldogs are prone to health issues. It's worth a think as pets will need vet care throughout their lives.

Ear Mites, Ticks, and Fleas

7

I t is common for dogs to get fleas as they can be anywhere. They can catch fleas or ear mites from other animals. Sometimes they can catch fleas just out on a walk. Ticks can also be found out in wooded areas or caught from other animals. Thankfully English Bulldogs have very short fur. So, you can usually see fleas and ticks more easily.

What is a flea?

Fleas are horrid little creatures that hop instead of flying. They drink the blood of the animal or human they hop onto. Some dogs can get anaemia or skin rashes from flea bites. In the summer, when it is warm, flea eggs hatch rapidly. If your dog catches fleas in the fall or winter, the flea eggs may hatch more quickly if you have the heating on in your home. When you first get your puppy or dog, ask your vet right away for the right flea treatment (puppies will need certain flea treatments as they are more sensitive.) This will prevent them from getting fleas from the get-go.

Signs your dog has fleas

- The most obvious sign is when your dog starts scratching their fur and cleaning themselves a lot.

- Some dogs get skin infections from allergies to fleas or from all of the scratching they are doing. English Bulldogs have sensitive skin and may be more prone to flea allergies.

- If you get a metal flea comb from the pet store, you can run with through your dog's fur. Usually, you will comb out the faeces of the flea which looks like little black flecks. If it is the flea itself, it will hop. Thankfully, English Bulldogs have super short hair.

- If you see jumping black dots in your dog's fur, they are fleas.

- Sometimes fleas go undetected until a bad infestation happens.

Fleas like to drink blood. After they drink blood, they lay eggs in your pet's fur and on furniture, carpets, and bedding.

More about fleas

Fleas like to drink blood. After they drink blood, they lay eggs in your pet's fur and on furniture, carpets, and bedding. They defaecate undigested food which are the little black flecks you will find in your dog's fur if they have fleas.

Fleas everywhere

Your home probably has fleas if your dog has them. Fleas grow in cycles from egg to larvae to pupae to the adult bouncing speck that is sucking blood from your beloved pet. So, it is important that you treat your home also to keep the cycle from spreading. Also, if you start your dog off with one of these preventatives it can stop the flea issue from happening in the first place. Just be sure NOT to apply a preventative immediately following a flea bath/dip and vice versa. Read the directions for each product to determine the amount of time to wait between products, as if you combine these too close to each other this can poison your Bulldog. They are very sensitive.

Here is what you need to do:

- As FRONTLINE is not absorbed into the body, it is considered one really great option for flea control for your dog. There is the regular FRONTLINE that kills fleas on your dog within 24 hours and kills ticks within 48 hours. If you repeat it monthly, then your dog should be flea and tick free. FRONTLINE Plus does the same thing but also stops flea eggs from hatching in your home! You need to use this monthly. It is very important to make sure the FRONTLINE you buy matches with your dog's weight. There are cheaper treatments that are not as effective as FRONTLINE and your problem can possibly continue. After you apply FRONTLINE don't touch your dog's neck until it dries.

- Also, keep cats away until it dries as the large dose a dog would use can be harmful to cats. Wash your hands right after applying FRONTLINE to your dog. Do not bather your dog for at least 48 hours after applying the FRONTLINE or it will be less effective.

- To get rid of adult fleas, eggs and larvae you need to wash your dog's bed with at least a 60-degree wash. You will need to do the same with soft toys, bedding, and other soft furnishings.

- While getting rid of the flea eggs, larvae, pupae and adult fleas in your home you will need to vacuum your chairs, carpets, and sofa once per day. Empty the vacuum bags into a plastic bag and tie it tight. Then put it in another bag and tie tightly so that nothing can get free.

- You can then purchase a flea spray for your home. Before spraying, make sure to take out any food or drink from the room you are spraying. There is a good spray called Acclaim which also kills dust mites and ticks. It is supposed to be very effective. Cheaper sprays often are not as effective. Also, open windows and air out the room for at least 15 -20 minutes before anyone goes back into the room.

You can also buy flea bombs. Once you have cleared a room you, set off the flea bomb. You cannot return to the room for at least two hours. Upon your return, you need to open every window to air out the room for a bit. Wipe off the flea bomb residue off of any furniture. Flea bombs will take care of a whole room, unlike sprays that can miss some spots.

- Make sure to groom your dog on a regular basis. Once you get rid of the fleas and start using flea control on a monthly basis, you will not need to use a flea comb and can just brush your dog regularly to keep their coat nice and reduce shedding. When your dog has fleas, you need to have your dog lay on a white sheet and slowly run the flea comb through their fur. Have a little bowl of soapy water nearby. If you get fleas on the comb, then dunk them in the soapy water. Mostly you will be brushing out flea faeces. Make sure to wash the sheet after in boiling hot water.

- 48 hours after you apply the FRONTLINE or other spot-on you can give your dog a bath to soothe their skin. Use lukewarm or cooler water for the bath as hot water can irritate skin further. There are special oatmeal dog baths you can give to soothe their skin. There are also dog grooming salons that will bathe your dog if you are not up for it.

Human flea bite treatment

Flea bites usually happen on people in exposed areas of the body such as hands, legs, feet, and ankles. You will have little red bumps, and your skin will itch. Clean the area with antiseptic. You can then put calamine lotion on the area to make the itching less severe. Some people have allergic reactions to flea bites. If it gets bad, then contact your GP.

Ticks

Ticks are much more dangerous than fleas for both humans and dogs as they can cause paralysis and Lyme disease. Ticks will latch on to any warm-blooded animal. They are usually found in wooded areas or plants and long grass. Ticks love to jump on unsuspecting animals and humans to feed on their blood. Ticks love to hide inside your English Bulldog's ears.

Search for ticks on your dog

- Ticks can be anywhere on your dog, but they like to go places that there is not a lot of hair mostly. Check inside and around your dog's ears, behind your dog's legs and under their armpits. One good habit to start is to give your dog a good rubdown as a treat rather than a food treat. If you do this regularly, you will find things you may not have otherwise as you will be used to your dog's body and what is normal and what is not. Definitely after walks in areas ticks may live, do a quick check. When you check under and in their ears, in addition to ticks, you can check for grass seeds (we discussed grass seeds previously) that can get deep into your dog's ears and sometimes even kill them.)

- A tick looks like a tiny dark bump on your dog that looks similar to a mole. At that point, you will see little brown legs sticking out, and their bodies swell and turn a pale shade of grey from all of the blood they have pulled out. If you see them before that phase, they look like a small skin-coloured mole.

- If you are using a medication like FRONTLINE then ticks are killed within 24 – 48 hours once they are on your dog. However, it is best to remove ticks as soon as they are seen to lessen the chance of disease transmission.

The process of removing ticks

- It is best to get a special tick removal tool to take ticks off of your beloved pet. You can use tweezers, but the special tools are more accurate. Do not try to just pull the tick out with your fingers or squeeze it. Also, do not burn the tick or put whiskey on it. Use the proper procedure.

- When you want to remove a tick from your dog (or yourself,) do it carefully as you do not want the tick's head to get stuck inside of you when you rip it off. Ticks like to get under your skin clockwise. Use your tool to grab the body of the tick and click anti-clockwise to make sure the head comes out with the body.

- Once the tick is removed you should squash it in a paper kitchen towel as you don't want it just hopping onto your dog again later. You can also flush it down the toilet. Clean the area where the tick was and apply special antiseptic cream for animals on the wound.

Ticks can be anywhere on your dog, but they like to go places that there is not a lot of hair mostly. Check inside and around your dog's ears, behind your dog's legs and under their armpits.

Worms

Puppies can easily pick up worms. Some are even born with them as they pick them up from their mother while they are still in her body. The website **www.vetbase.co.uk** advises that you worm puppies every two weeks from 4 weeks of age until they are 12 weeks old. After this, they should be treated monthly until they are six months of age. Then they can be wormed every three months, the same as an adult dog.

There are three options for worming depending on your pup's age:

- Tablets are used most often. You need to follow the instructions or ask your vet for advice as to how many worm pills to give based on their age and weight. If you are unsure at all, please call your vet's office. If you overdose a small pup on wormer, they can get very ill.

- Liquid form. This is not used as often but is available and follow the instructions just as you would with tablets.

- Spot-on wormers. These days there are spot-on wormers for those who don't want to deal with administering pills. Be sure to follow the instruction based on the weight and age of your dog.

Dreaded ear mites

If your English Bulldog is shaking their head, they may have ear mites or an ear infection. Your vet needs to check your dog's ears and might even need to take a scraping to look under a microscope to confirm ear mites. Also, ask your vet to check for grass seeds. Grass seeds are very dangerous in ears. Usually, your vet will have you clean their ears with a special ear cleaner and use special ear mite medicines if the diagnosis is, indeed, ear mites.

There are also flea and tick treatments that help prevent most ear mites. Check with your veterinarian. Ear mites can spread to your other pets. So, if you have other pets make sure to treat them also.

Pet Insurance

Pet insurance is very popular these days as it can cover those high-priced illnesses or incidents that come along that can be difficult for the average person to afford unexpectedly. There are many pets given up to rescue centres because their owners simply cannot afford them. Imagine your dog needs surgery and it is thousands of pounds. If you have pet insurance that covers the surgery, it can be a relief. Otherwise, you have some hard decisions to make if you cannot afford it. English Bulldogs are prone to so many health issues that pet insurance seriously needs to be considered.

Pros of obtaining pet insurance

There are a lot of great reasons to purchase pet insurance. We have some listed here:

- Pet insurance can give you some peace of mind. If your dog unexpectedly needs major surgery or gets a serious injury, the cost will be covered by pet insurance.

- Any ongoing conditions your dog gets after you start the insurance will be covered up to the highest amount offered in your policy.

- There are some pet insurance policies that cover if your dog is the cause of a car accident and will pay to repair the driver's car and handle personal injuries the driver may have. These policies can be more expensive but are something to look into.

- For pups from the age of 6 weeks, you can get special puppy insurance.

- If you keep up your payments for your pet insurance, your dog will be covered for life which will cover any vet bills allowed in the policy.

- Some pet insurance providers will cover alternative remedies such as acupuncture and herbal medicine.

- If you insure more than one pet, you might be entitled to a discount for pet insurance.

Some pet insurance providers will cover alternative remedies such as acupuncture and herbal medicine.

Cons of obtaining pet insurance

- You can possibly charged more for older dogs.

- Certain breeds that need special care might be charged more for. Usually, English Bulldogs are not in this list of breeds.

- Some pet insurance charges more for un-neutered or un-spayed dogs as they can have more health issues as discussed in our spay and neuter section.

- Many pet insurers do not cover pre-existing conditions for around 12 months before you purchased the policy. So, if your dog had any symptoms of a disease or condition or your vet advised they had a condition during that time they might not cover it. Speak with the insurer to go over this portion to make sure you understand what is covered or not.

- It is usual for a lot of pet insurance companies to not pay for any injuries or illnesses that occur during the first 14 days of coverage.

Different kinds of policies

There are usually three different types of pet insurance:

- Coverage for the life of your pet – This coverage covers the most illnesses and will cover them for the life of your pet.

- Policy per condition – This is a limited policy and will only cover a condition until the limit has been met. You cannot later claim for the condition again.

- A yearly policy – These policies only cover one year at a time, and there is a set amount you can claim per condition. Any treatment beyond that fixed amount, you will need to pay for. Also, per condition, you can claim only one time. If your dog ends up with a long-term illness, this policy is not for you. All in all, the safest policy is the one with lifelong coverage.

What is the best deal?

There are so many providers on the market at this time. It is worth your time to contact at least a few insurers and compare prices and coverage. Also, ask friends and your vet for recommendations. A few popular plans are Direct Line Pet Insurance, Petplan, Animal Friends, John Lewis Finance Pet Insurance, and PDSA. **www.confused.com** is a good place to compare quotes if you do not want to contact each provider individually. You can also compare at **www.petinsuranceonline.co.uk** to check different categories of coverage.

What to ask pet insurance companies

Potential pet insurance companies can send you a document showing you what will be covered. If you do not understand the policy or have questions you need to always feel free to ask. Some possible questions that may help are:

Q. What is covered in my policy?

A. Never assume a thing when it comes to pet insurance. There are cheaper plans that can end up being of very little value to the pet owner in the long run. Ask if your insurer covers more than vet bills. Some will cover fees to board your dog at a kennel or compensate you if your dog gets ill and your holiday has to be cancelled.

Also, some policies cover 'third party liability.' This is helpful if your pet is the cause of any accident your dog causes that results in property damage or death. Usually, your pet insurance will pay your legal fees and will compensate the party that is suing you. There is often an excess applied to a lot of the claims you make.

Q. Is this policy a 'covered for life' policy?

A. With the 'covered for life' policy any long-term illness will be covered over and over. However, there is a limit to how much they pay out each year. This is the most complete kind of pet insurance but also the most costly. If this is what you are looking for, make sure to confirm it with the insurer. As we mentioned before, English Bulldogs are prone to some health issues such as major respiratory problems, severe skin allergies, arthritis, overheating, acne, eczema, dry skin, hip dysplasia, degenerative spine disease, idiopathic head tremors, cherry eye, joint, and ligament injuries, vomiting, regurgitation, heart disease, fold dermatitis, Brachycephalic Airway Syndrome, and vaccination sensitivity. English Bulldogs also have the highest rate of cancer of most breeds. It would be good to have your pet insured before anything like this can possibly show up. These things happen, and it is good to be prepared. It might be a smart to consider the 'covered for life' policy if you can afford it, especially before anything comes up due to pre-existing conditions not always being covered in some policies.

Q. What is not covered in my policy?

A. Ask what is not covered. Some policies will only pay for a condition once per year. Others will only reimburse for the first year of your dog's sickness. For long-term illnesses this would not be ideal.

Q. No matter what treatment really costs, will this policy only pay for a certain percentage for some illnesses?

A. It is important to ask this. The surgery may cost £2000. However, your insurer may only pay out £1200. Do not assume that every pound is paid out.

Q. What is the process for making a claim for vet's fees?

A. With most pet insurance you pay the vet, and the insurer reimburses you via a claim form. There are some insurance companies that will let your vet directly bill them. Your policy should list this procedure.

More About English Bulldogs

What can I say? English Bulldogs are social butterflies in a stocky frame that capture the hearts of almost everyone they meet. They have a low energy level but still need exercise daily. They can learn to be friends with many different kinds of animals such as farm animals, rabbits, and guinea pigs. English Bulldogs are cool dogs. They need minimal grooming, and they are loving companions. English Bulldogs are especially caring and loving with children, older people, dogs, and other animals. English Bulldogs love their people!

Be a responsible dog owner

You need to keep control of your dog per the laws of the land. The law is also very concerned if your dog bites a human being. If your dog is prone to being aggressive, you need to not only take it to a behaviourist, but you need to make sure your dog is not let loose where it can be in danger of being aggressive to people or other dogs. It's very serious if your dog attacks a person and bad if it attacks another dog. Also, when out on walks, make sure to pick up your dog's poop. Always have little baggies ready.

Stolen or lost dogs

If your dog does go missing, it can have you frantic. Hopefully, you will have microchipped your dog and put a collar with a name/number tag on your pooch. If your dog goes missing:

- Look for your dog in all of the places they love to go, such as favourite walking spots.

- Call all vets in the area you live in. Sometimes people take dogs they find into vets.

- Call or go down to the Dog Warden Service for your area.

- Go door to door with a picture of your dog asking if anyone has seen it. Bring slips of paper with your phone number to give them if they do.

- Make some 'LOST DOG' posters, preferably with a photo of your dog. Now that you are reading this, if you have not already, take some good photos of your dog. Also, add the word 'REWARD' and do not specify the amount. If you are on a budget, a reward can be £20. It seems people pay more attention to the word REWARD in all caps. I once found an elderly woman's dog after seeing a poster. I did not accept the reward and was just happy for her to be with her dog. So, some people may not even take the money.

> If your dog is prone to being aggressive, you need to not only take it to a behaviourist, but you need to make sure your dog is not let loose where it can be in danger of being aggressive to people or other dogs.

- Call the police! Sometimes people bring lost dogs to the police station as there are scanners for microchips there.

- Place an advertisement in your local paper as ask local shops if you can pop a lost dog poster in their window on or their noticeboard.

- There are websites such as **www.dogslost.co.uk** where you can register that you have lost your dog. **www.nationalpetsregister.org** is another pet registry you can use (the UK National Pets Register.) Animal shelters, vets, police and ordinary folks across the UK check there daily. These are both free services.

- Make sure to have an updated nametag on your dog's collar with name and phone number. You can also include an address. These times are when it is good to have spent the small amount to microchip your dog for peace of mind.

Adopting a dog

You can sometimes find English Bulldogs at rescue centres or special English Bulldog breed rescues that would love a home with you. It is always worth thinking about adopting a dog rather than buying one. Visit your local rescue centre to see if they have any English Bulldogs available. Many times, people cannot keep up with the time needed for a English Bulldog and give them up. If you are game for it, then you might be this dog's dream home. You will find English Bulldogs at breed-specific rescues.

Adopting a dog will usually involve an adoption fee to cover costs and help the other homeless animals. You will be asked a lot of questions, but that is good for the animal being adopted as they can make sure you and the dog you want will be a good fit. Most rescues will do a check of your home to make sure it is a good place for the dog you are adopting. Many times, just agreeing to the home check shows you are serious. During home checks, rescues can also give suggestions for things you can do to make sure your English Bulldog will be healthy, happy and safe.

Travelling with your English Bulldog

Many people tend to have a dog-sitter come to their home to care for their dog, or they take their dog to kennels when they are going away on a trip. However, sometimes people want to take their dog with them. Others are moving permanently and, of course, want to take their dog to their new home. Keep in mind that many airlines now forbid brachycephalic breeds, also known as short-faced or snub-nosed dogs, from their planes. The reason being that many snub-faced dogs have died on flights due to their breathing issues. So, your English Bulldog may not be allowed on the plane. Here are a few tips below.

Kennels and dog-sitters

- Ask people you trust for recommendations for a good pet-sitter or kennels.

- A Pet-sitter will be coming into your home. You need someone trustworthy. Make sure the pet sitter is insured for liability, including care, custody, and control of your dog. Make sure to get a signed copy of your pet-sitting contract with the pet-sitter. Make sure the pet-sitter knows pet first aid and has a backup plan in case they have a personal emergency.

- For kennels, you need to check that they are licensed and insured for liability, including care, custody, and control of your dog. Also, visit the facility to see where your dog will be staying. Ask the kennels how many walks your dog will have and how much attention your dog will receive. Ask if there is a discount on price if you provide your dog's food. It is good to keep your dog on the same food to not have too many changes at once while you are gone. Your dog will need to be vaccinated against kennel cough before boarding. Remember, Egnlish Bulldogs are very sensitive to this vaccine. So, you might want to consider a house-sitter to come stay with your dog.

- If you decide on using a kennel, then bring your dog's favourite blanket, food, and toys, so they have familiar items with them in their new environment. This will help ease stress for your dog.

- Make sure either the kennel or pet-sitter has a print-out for what to do if your English Bulldog falls ill with heat exhaustion. Some people might think to rush to the vet first without cooling the dog down first.

Flying with your English Bulldog

If you do decide to fly with your dog, you need to plan ahead of time. Keep in mind that quite a few snub-faced dogs, including English Bulldogs, have died on flights due to their breathing issues. To make things simple, you can use an agency that helps fly pets. They will do a lot of the work for you and guide you through everything for a fee. If the fee is affordable, this can be good for someone pressed with time. No matter what, check the regulations of your airline about flying snub-faced dogs. In 2004 The Pet Travel Scheme was introduced to stop pets from having to go through the stress of quarantine if certain requirements were met. This scheme only has certain countries participating such as the UK and the EU. There are certain time schedules for vaccinations, and pet passports so plan well ahead. For more information on the travel scheme, please go to this website **https://www.gov.uk/take-pet-abroad** and this website **http://apha.defra. gov.uk/external-operations-admin/library/documents/exports/ET159.pdf**.

Dog-friendly holidays

Two great websites to find information about dog-friendly accommodation are **www.dogfriendlybritain.co.uk** and **http://www.officialpethotels.com**. Sometimes you will need to pay for your dog to stay in holiday accommodation. However, many places it's free.

English Bulldogs – Your Loyal Companion For Life

The English Bulldog is extremely loyal and devoted to its people. A Bulldog is happy when there is family around to give them affection, and they love to be around the daily activities. You can have acres of playland, lots of exercise, and a zillion toys but an English Bulldog without its family is an unhappy dog. The English Bulldog is the ideal companion, always ecstatic to see you and he is happy when you are happy. Try doing exercises on the ground, bring in shopping from the car, having a kip on the couch or do chores around the house; you will never have to do those things on your own again with this constant companion. An English Bulldog wants to be involved in your activities and be a part of it all.

Do not be harsh with them or it can really affect them badly. You do, however, need to be consistent and firm with them throughout their lives as they are known to test boundaries. As they are so people-oriented, it is cruel to leave them alone for long periods of time. If left alone too much they can become very unhappy and destructive. As they are highly adaptable and low energy, they can live just as easily in a house as an apartment as long as they are given the proper amount of exercise daily and the right amount of mental stimulation. These are pretty awesome dogs. If you are looking to adopt or buy an English Bulldog, we hope this book has helped in your decision-making process. If you have already adopted an English Bulldog, we hope this information was helpful, and you enjoy having your new faithful friend in your home.

The English Bulldog is extremely loyal and devoted to its people. A Bulldog is happy when there is family around to give them affection, and they love to be around the daily activities.